PUBLIC SPEAKING

Manage Business Presentations by Learning Storytelling Techniques and Overcome Your Fear of Public Speaking Overnight

(Techniques to Overcome Anxiety and Improve Speaking Skills)

James C. Reynolds

Published by Rob Miles

© **James C. Reynolds**

All Rights Reserved

Conversation Skills: Manage Business Presentations by Learning Storytelling Techniques and Overcome Your Fear of Public Speaking Overnight (Techniques to Overcome Anxiety and Improve Speaking Skills)

ISBN 978-1-989990-02-5

All rights reserved. No part of this guide may be reproduced in any form without permission in writing from the publisher except in the case of brief quotations embodied in critical articles or reviews.

Legal & Disclaimer

The information contained in this book is not designed to replace or take the place of any form of medicine or professional medical advice. The information in this book has been provided for educational and entertainment purposes only.

The information contained in this book has been compiled from sources deemed reliable, and it is accurate to the best of the Author's knowledge; however, the Author cannot guarantee its accuracy and validity and cannot be held liable for any errors or omissions. Changes are periodically made to this book. You must consult your doctor or get professional medical advice before using any of the suggested remedies, techniques, or information in this book.

Upon using the information contained in this book, you agree to hold harmless the Author from and against any damages, costs, and expenses, including any legal fees potentially resulting from the application of any of the information provided by this guide. This disclaimer applies to any damages or injury caused by the use and application, whether directly or indirectly, of any advice or information presented, whether for breach of contract, tort, negligence, personal injury, criminal intent, or under any other cause of action.

You agree to accept all risks of using the information presented inside this book. You need to consult a professional medical practitioner in order to ensure you are both able and healthy enough to participate in this program.

Table of Contents

INTRODUCTION 1

CHAPTER 1: IN THE BEGINNING 3

CHAPTER 2: BEFORE THE PRESENTATION DAY 10

CHAPTER 3: BODY LANGUAGE: POSTURE, FACIAL EXPRESSION, GESTURES... 23

CHAPTER 4: YOUR BODY 43

CHAPTER 5: MINDSET 57

CHAPTER 6: NLP TECHNIQUES CAN HELP YOU OVERCOME YOUR PUBLIC SPEAKING FEAR 72

CHAPTER 7: HOW TO OVERCOME STAGE FRIGHT 85

CHAPTER 8: ACTIONS SPEAK AS LOUD AS YOUR WORDS. 91

CHAPTER 9: HOW TO WOW YOUR AUDIENCE 98

CHAPTER 10: THE HEART OF THE MIND: 102

CHAPTER 11: BECOMING THE BEST SPEAKER 127

CHAPTER 12: AUDIENCE TOOLS - HOW TO USE VOICE TONE AND PAUSE 133

CHAPTER 13: DELIVER YOUR FIRST SPEECH 144

CHAPTER 14: OTHER FACTORS TO CONSIDER IN SPEECH PREPARATION 152

CHAPTER 15: PROMOTING YOUR BUSINESS 164

CHAPTER 16: PUBLIC SPEAKING – HOW TO APPEARAND BE CONFIDENT ONSTAGE 171

CHAPTER 17: TIPS FOR PUBLIC SPEAKING 175

CHAPTER 18: IMPROMPTU SPEAKING & HOW TO TELL A TALL TALE 182

CONCLUSION 190

Introduction

This book contains proven steps and strategies on how to develop unstoppable confidence speaking in front of large groups of people.

In today's society the ability to communicate your message is not something we all should learn… it is something we all MUST learn, if we want to be a happy, and successful member of society. For many people however, the thought of speaking in front of a large group of people terrifies them.

It's time to become the speaker, leader, and champion you were meant to be. Whether you are a decent speaker already, or a terrified newbie, this book will take your speaking to the next level.

Thanks again for downloading this book, I hope you enjoy it!

Chapter 1: In the Beginning

If you assume that you can lace up your shoes and just head out and bust out that 26 mile run on your first try, you are sorely mistaken. (You will also be ridiculously sore.) In the beginning of any superhero's story is his backstory and for you, Super Marathon Runner, the backstory is called the fundamentals. They call them that because they are no fun and you have to be pretty mental to want to keep on going after you find out what is in store for you. Let's get going.

Tell me Your Why:

Running a marathon is not just about getting up and going one day- there is a reason. If you only have one reason behind your run you are less likely to complete the task especially when it gets harder and less pleasant.

Your goal should not be too simplistic- "I want to run far." " I want to lose weight."

Your goal should not be overly complicated- "I want to run this marathon and capture America's heart in the process!"

Your goal should be realistic- "I want to finish this race." "I want to be in better shape than when I started."

Your goal should be definable- "I want to finish this race." "I want to be in better shape than when I started" (See a pattern, here?).

Your goal should be realistic- " I want to lose 20 pounds during training"

Well-defined, achievable goals will not only keep you on track but will allow you to break them into smaller goals. Your first goal is to start with your training and figure out where you are so that you can work from there.

Tell me Where You are Right Now:

When is the last time that you ran? I don't mean the time that you heard the ice cream man or that time that you shagged fanny to catch the last bus. I mean when is the last time that you ran and really meant to be running? If your answer is never, then you are a true beginner. If your answer was not in the last year or so, you should also count yourself as a beginner.

Now, thinking of that last time that you ran- how did you feel? Were you gasping and out of breath in the first mile or did you push yourself to three or four miles? Think of yourself as an intermediate if you said yes to the push.

Regardless of that last run, the only way to determine where you are right now is to run. Don't worry about time, length, distance or speed just yet. Just warm up a little bit and then run. Stop and evaluate how you feel. After some rest, it is time to really assess where you are and this is where your gadgets will come in handy- in this case you will need either a heart rate monitor or something to track your distance, speed and time. (Lots of options for smart phones, here and many of them are free which is great if you are not an eccentric billionaire at the moment.) For this run you are going to see how far you can go and how fast. You can take walking breaks if you need to but keep track of how long you can run without stopping. The ultimate goal before even starting your marathon training is to be able to run non-stop for thirty minutes straight. (We will get into more about heart rate zones later.)

Do You Know how to Run?

Sure, that sounds like an easy question, but it really isn't. If you do not know how to run with proper form you are going to either never progress beyond where you are now, or you are going to injure yourself. Either way, you won't be making your goal of running a marathon, will you?

Proper form starts with a relaxed stance. If you have tension in your face, neck and shoulders it will be a drain on your precious energy. If you are tensing your legs, that will also waste energy. Even worse than wasting energy though- you are creating rigid areas where injury is just begging to happen. Don't lock your jaw. Don't lock your knees. Don't clench your fists. (Superheroes who shout "why you!" and then race off after the bad guy with their fists already clenched are absolutely NOT planning on running a marathon!)

Don't be anti-gravity man. When a child is first learning how to walk or run they lean forward and off they go. For the most part their parents are gritting their teeth convinced their little darling is going to bash their bean at a moment's notice and become the Concussion Kid. But, kids being kids will not even pay their parents any attention and they just run and run like drunken sailors on their first day of shore leave. Once we hit adulthood the fear of the pavement becomes palpable, and we are fighting against gravity with our every step. We hold our shoulders back, tummies in and neck held high because we think this is how we are supposed to stand and to run. And who told us that? Probably some dastardly villain who wants to make us pretty bad at running is who. Learning how to lean into the run is a vital key to not only running farther and faster, but to making the run feel easier as well. Let's face it, if running felt less like work and more like play, a lot more of us would do it.

So, you have set a goal (hopefully one that is meaningful, realistic and attainable) and have reviewed proper running form as well as assessing your current run level. We are ready to gear up before that first big run!

Pro-tip: If you can have someone videotape a short run, you can analyze your form and make improvements. Even better: go to one of the race form clinics and have a real professional do it for you!

Chapter 2: Before the presentation day

What steps you should follow before the presentation day?

Step #1 Preparation before the presentation.

Preparation, then Preparation, then Preparation. Preparation for the presentation is the most important part when you are going to conduct. Presentation is not only means PowerPoint presentation. Presentation is very wide and it is wider that PowerPoint presentations. It can be an interview, minister speech for an issue, Professor in the university, teacher in class ...etc.

We will guide you through this book on how to prepare and the secrets behind the presentation success.

Step #2 Preparation more for shorter presentations.

Mark Twain (an American author and humorist) said a very interesting quote. He said "If you want me to give you a two-hour presentation, I am ready today. If you want only a five-minute speech, it will take me two weeks to prepare".

You should prepare yourself for the time boundaries of your presentation. The shorter duration that was planned for the presentation, the more effort you will spend to prepare for the presentation.

Step #3 Follow the PASS model.

What is the PASS model?

The "**P**urpose **A**udience **S**tructure **S**tyle" model is the best model that a presenter should follow to conduct his presentation to the audience.

In the following steps we will guide you through how to prepare for the presentation purpose followed by audience control followed by building structure for the presentation and finally control your style and presentation style.

Step #4 Remove the fear from your audience.

Fear from audience is definitely will make you fail in the presentation. If you didn't get rid of your fear you will lose control and forget everything.

Holding a fear inside you like holding a chair above your head. Can you continue the presentation with the chair above your head?? Of course not, you must drop the chair down and get rid of your fear.

You can overcome your fear by asking yourself:

what could happen if I failed in the presentation and didn't present it will?

You will be asked to do it again later … It is OK

You will be fired … of course not

You will be embarrassed … so what !!

And all these will not happen if you prepared well from the beginning.

Step #5 Include all possible senses in the presentation.

There is a tale says:

I hear -- I forget

I see with my eyes -- I remember

I do it myself -- I understand

So it is important for the presenter (especially if the presentation is a training session) to stick to the previous tale to make sure that the audience got the presented information.

How we learn?

The next graph shows the differences between our 5 senses information perception:

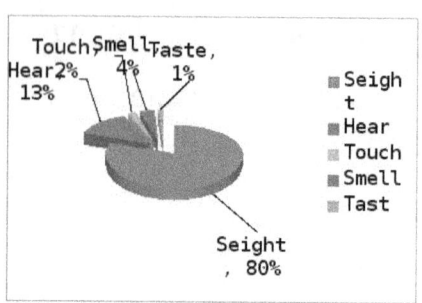

As you can see through the Pie chart, people have different perception from their senses.

And by experienced practices we concluded that after 5 days:

People retain about 10% from what they listen through their ears.

People retain about 30 % from what they watch through their eyes.

But people retain more than 60 % from what they watch and listen.

Therefore, Presenter should include all possible senses in his presentation.

Step #6 Know the purpose behind the presentation.

When you are going to conduct a presentation you should care about your audience and firstly collect information about:

What is the presentation purpose?

It is very important for the presenter to make sure that the goal of the presentation is kept in the audience mind after the presentation ends.

Understanding the purpose of the presentation is the key for its success.

Why am I conducting this presentation?

1- Is it awareness of something new "like new ISO 9001 version"? or,

2- Giving training session to students or,

3- Explaining current crisis to the top management level or company CEO.

4- Is it for motivating some workers?

It is really different and keeping this concept in your mind during the whole presentation is very important.

When you understand the purpose of the presentation you are going to act, stand, behave and speak with a tone related to the presentation goal which is a tone expected from your audience.

Step #7 Know your audience before the presentation.

How many people will attend my presentation?

Your audience are 2 ,10 ,or thousands!!

Because in large audiences, you will prepare for using microphone and your movement style on the stage ... etc.

In few audiences you will concentrate on power point show and other convincing strategies.

What are the ages of your audience?

You are going to make the presentation in front of kids (10 to 13 years old) or the audience is university students, or it is a group of scientists!!

Example:

Imagine you are going to make a presentation for 11 years old kids in a school for what is the air conditioner?

Do you think they will be interested to know how the refrigeration circuit works using the "fluid mechanics engineering"!! Or how could the "Enthalpy" affect the evaporator coil performance!! .. Of course not.

They will be interested in:

How colder the air conditioner could cool the air?

What is the basic knowledge of the air conditioner and its parts and simple drawing for the unit?

You should think in their minds and give them the content they understand according to their mentality.

In contrary, giving the above mentioned presentation about the "Air Conditioner" to a group of engineers, you will present the issue with complicated graphs and equations and go deep in.

Same concept applies when you present issue to a higher level like your boss or your management.

What are the interests of your audience?

Knowing the interests of your audience is essential for your presentation success.

Example:

You are going to give a presentation to soccer players about "medical protection for injuries".

Do you think the players will be interested in knowing the types of medical treatments and their effective material name and the details of the enzymes on their bodies? .. Of course not.

They will be interested in how to take care while playing and what kind of basic actions to take firstly when the injury occurs until the medical team arrives because more scientific information is not the player's job.

What is the level of education of your audience?

You should know who you are talking to,

Are you going to speak:

To your boss or,

Giving presentation to your instructor about what you had learned or,

You are presenting your PHD to your PHD committee,

all of the above are completely different from:

Giving presentation to some school kids (lower level of education).

In the first case you should take care of all words you are saying and even every single equation you are going to use in the presentation.

What is the culture of your audience?

Some habits and traditions have different meanings in different countries.

Example:

In India when somebody shakes his neck to the right and to the left it means "Yes"!! While in many other countries in the world it means "NO", so if you are giving a presentation in India and someone asks you a question and you want to say yes (take care).

Study the culture of your audience very well before the presentation and if you don't have enough information just search in google and you will find good information.

Step #8 Know what to wear before presentation

You should know the type of clothes you will wear before the presentation.

For men:

Using the formal dark suits will give you more authority in the presentation, thus more confidence.

If it is not formal presentation, light color suits are friendlier than the dark suits.

Don't wear multi color tie. This will distract the audience attention. Your tie should be tied well.

Avoid wearing shoes with multiple colors.

For women:

Formal Black or gray or navy suit would be the best. Always choose darker colors.

Blazers with coordinated skirts are good.

Avoid wearing attractive necklace, earrings and bracelets because this will distract the audience attention.

Hair style should be suitable.

Chapter 3: Body Language: Posture, Facial Expression, Gestures...

As mentioned in the first chapter, body language is essential to the delivery of a clear, trustworthy message. For that purpose, it's imperative to work hard in order to master the different expressions of your body language. Accordingly, you should strive to master the power of communication through your body language.

This will include:

- How to sit/ stand while presenting or public speaking.

- How to move your body, head, and arms.

- Which posture is right, which is wrong.

- Facial expressions.

1- Relaxing your body and face

A- A relaxed body posture

A relaxed body posture attests to one's confidence, and confidence bespeaks trust and power.

Shoulders and the upper body

To maintain a relaxed body posture, let your upper body rest in a well-balanced manner above the pelvis.

Body Language-

You can also let it drop slightly to one side. Don't tense up your shoulders. Instead, open your chest gracefully, pull your shoulders back and let them rest down loosely.

Arms and hands

Whenever we are nervous, our arms tend to move suddenly in a disjointed manner. Let your arms hang loosely or move them smoothly. Crossing the arms indicates some tension. Folding the arms may be just comfortable enough.

Use your hands to enhance what you are saying. Let them gently shape ideas in the air, not in a sudden or tensed manner.

Legs and the lower body

Let your feet rest lightly on the floor. You may cross them but never wind them around each other. Be careful: when you make an effort to look relaxed by controlling the upper body and the arms, the legs are automatically held tense, showing hidden tension.

Your body posture depends as well on the kind of programme, and the content of the programme you are presenting. While an entertaining programme with a casual concept can be done with a casual posture, the more serious the programme and its content the more assertive the posture should be.

Exercise #1: Body Posture

Because your posture attests your confidence and is crucially important to your presenting and public

speaking career, you should be able to effortlessly and naturally maintain it while on podium or stage. To naturally maintain this confident posture, you have to adopt it throughout your everyday routine. It should become your usual posture.

In order to achieve this, practise this exercise every morning:

Before getting out of the house, stand straight, your back pressed to the wall, push your shoulders back. Naturally and effortlessly press them against the wall. Feel yourself taller than you really are, like something is pulling your lower back all along to the shoulders, and up towards the roof. Do it again during the day, whenever you notice your back crawling down again.

B-A relaxed face

Your face is the main sign of your relaxation or, on the contrary, your tension. When you're relaxed on the inside, your face will naturally mirror this relaxation and confidence on the outside. However, there are a few guidelines for proper face expressions and movements.

Mouth

When talking, open your mouth moderately. Move your lips neither with small movements nor with large movements. Open it just wide enough to allow proper articulation.

Eyes

Look directly into your audience/ guest's eyes, with just a little blinking. Do not scare them with deep

Body Language-

staring, nor give them an exaggeratedly doe-eyed look. Keep your eyebrows stable or move them with speech, but don't frown.

Head movements

When you move your head, move it smoothly and in time with your speaking and other expressions.

2- Using your body as a communication tool

So far, we've talked about the appropriate body posture. In the coming paragraphs, you will learn how to use your body language to emphasise the content you're transmitting, and how to intensify the words that need to be intensified using your body language.

Head

While on camera, most of the time it is only your head that is in view. Move it naturally in association with your words. Twist, turn and nod your head in harmony with the content of the words you're saying.

The importance of synchronization

However, while emphasising using two elements, the voice and the body, beware of sending out mixed messages. For example, you can't emphasise with your words while keeping your head, body and face motionless. When you're welcoming your guest, you can't tell him 'It's good to have you on the show' while standing rigidly, with a neutral facial expression. The basic rule for using your body to emphasise is to synchronise, to make everything act together: words and intonation, as well as all the bits of your body that you are using to support the emphasis.

-Own The Spotlights

Eye contact

As a public speaker, you have to establish a powerful connection with a significant number of listeners, during a limited time sequence. As a TV presenter, you're sitting miles away from the target viewers. In both cases, the most powerful tool at your disposal to establish a connection with the viewers is, without doubt, your eyes: the frequency and time of eye contact, eyebrow movement, or purposeful blinking.

The frequency and time of eye contact also vary according to the kind of programme presented. The content, mood and concept of the programme must be taken into consideration as well. Proper and timely eyebrow movements also enhance a presentation to a large extent. A news anchor, for example, should maintain persistent and confident eye contact with viewers. Persistence hooks their attention. Confidence gives them the feeling that he's transmitting accurate, trustworthy information. Prompt eyebrow movements are extremely important for expressing the seriousness, formality and importance of the news being transmitted.

On the other hand, the TV presenter of an entertainment programme can have more relaxed, more friendly eye contact with his viewers. His eyes should sparkle and smile every time he meets with his audience. He's there to befriend them, have fun with them and entertain them.

During an interview, your eyes should connect with those of your guest. He should feel that you are giving

him 100 percent of your attention. Otherwise he might lose his concentration, get more anxious, and ramble more. Keep in mind that your guest is not necessarily an expert in public speaking. Make him feel you're with him, leading him every step of the way. Assure him with your eyes that you're ready to intervene if he should panic or lose track of the idea he's developing.

On the other hand, connect with your audience gently, by a glance at the camera, or at the studio guests in case you're having an in-studio audience. Make brief eye contact every now and then, to ensure that they are listening and to make them feel they're also part of the conversation.

Hands

Just as in real life and in daily conversations, on TV and while public speaking, hand gestures are a complementary communication tool that helps us express ourselves, in addition to words. When we're passionate about a subject, we intend to use more gestures to express our passion. An explanatory content requires intensive hand movements. An enthusiastic entertainment programme or a sports show, requires complementary enthusiastic hand gestures. The more you feel the need to explain yourself, the more your hand gestures will naturally become accentuated.

While a viewer is talking, whether he's part of an in-studio audience or a phone-in caller, move or lean a little towards the camera. This gives the impression that you leaned towards them so as to give them your full attention. Nod to encourage agreement or to show attentiveness. Move your hands a little towards them, as if wanting to give something or to reach out to them.

Don't be frightened of using stronger emphasis whenever the topic requires it, and whenever you want to overtly show your energy and passion about a point. You should also synchronise your words with the emphasis. In that case use power words, speaking them a little more loudly with more energy and passion. If you are truly passionate about what you're saying, make no mistake, you will make the audience passionate about it. They will hear it in your words, feel it in your body, see it in your eyes.

Big-emphasis body language includes slightly bigger gestures, wide, sweeping arm movements, nodding your head more, moving about the stage (if you're standing on stage and have enough liberty to move). You might as well create contrast, sometimes being stationary, and then moving suddenly. This catches the attention of the audience, who would have been restless for a while.

Repeated moves

A boxer can win with a knockout blow or, more likely, with repeated blows that wear his opponent down. The same effect is created with big emphasis. Rhythmic action also taps into primitive senses and can create an almost hypnotic effect.

3- Bringing the interview to life using body language

The importance of body language goes further than shoring up your conviction in the messages you're transmitting. It's the key to a real connection with your guests and your audience. Investing in proper body language upgrades your show to another level, a level where the studio becomes no less than an extension into your viewers' living rooms. It makes you build a connection with your guest and therefore with your audience and thus creates in the audience a fantasy about having a real connection with you and brings your guests closer to reality. Your show becomes so familiar that it feels like a casual visit you and your guests are paying to your audience at home.

Now, let's put the words we have been bandying about into practice, to find out how exactly you can use your body language to express your ideas more firmly and built a connection with your guests and audience.

A- While you're talking

- Move towards your guests and audience when stating important points.

- Reach out towards them, palms curved and up or towards one another, as if giving them something.

- Use a simulated embrace, curving your arms with palms inwards as if hugging them. Make sure not to

-Own The Spotlights

overuse those gestures though. Use them only when they serve the subject at hand.

- Make unblinking eye contact, gazing directly at them (particularly transitioning from no eye contact).

- Use 'doe eyes' to project passion for the person or idea at hand.

B- While your guest or audience is talking

- You want to be attentive. An attentive head may be tilted slightly forward towards the guest or the audience speaking. It may also show curiosity when tilted to the side. Sometimes this may, however, indicate uncertainty. An attentive person looks at the other person without taking their gaze away. They will likely blink less, almost for fear of missing something.

- Ignore distractions.

- Stillness: Body movement often betrays distracting thoughts and feelings. When the listener is largely still, the implication is that everything else has been forgotten except the other person, with not even internal dialogue or thoughts being allowed to distract (even though actually you should be thinking of the next logical question).

- Patience: When you want to hear more from the other person you are patient, listening until they have finished speaking and not butting in with your views.

Body Language-

Even when you have something to say or when they pause, you still patiently seek a full understanding of them and give them space in which to complete what they have to say. Once you feel they've clearly stated their point, you can than intervene to move the dialogue on to the next logical question.

• Open body: Open body language shows that you are not feeling defensive, and that you are mentally open to what the audience/guest have to say (and hence not closed to their thoughts).

• Slow nodding: Nodding shows agreement and also encourages the other person to keep talking. Fast nodding may show impatience, whilst slower nodding indicates understanding and approval.

• Interest noises: Little noises such as 'uh huh' and 'mmm' show that you are interested, understand and want to hear more. They thus encourage the other person to open up and reveal more.

- Reflecting: When you reflect the other person back to them they feel affirmed and that you are aligned with them. Reflecting activities range from matching body language to paraphrasing what they say.

4- The common mistakes to avoid

When it comes to body language, simply avoiding

the most common mistakes and replacing them with

more confident movements will make a big difference.

Train yourself to avoid the common mistakes mentioned

-Own The Spotlights

below, and you'll see that simple changes can make all the difference.

Common mistake #1- Avoiding eye contact

Avoiding eye contact may indicate a lack of confidence. You may seem stressed or unprepared.

What to do instead: The vast majority of beginner TV presenters spend far too much time looking down at notes. Spend 90 per cent or more of your show time switching your eye contact from your guest to your audience and back.

Common mistake #2- Slouching

Slouching points towards an un-authoritative character, and signals a lack of confidence.

What to do instead: Don't use a tabletop or podium as an excuse to lean on it. Sit or stand in a relaxed manner, just like you stand at the main door of your house to greet a guest coming over for a visit. Maintain this welcoming, interested, standing or sitting posture throughout your conversation with your guest, and your interaction with your audience.

Common mistake #3- Fidgeting

Fidgeting is more likely the posture of a nervous, unsure and unprepared person.

What to do instead: You can stop fidgeting by eventually learning to move with purpose, as we've mentioned earlier in this chapter.

Body Language-

Common mistake #4- Using phony gestures

Phony gestures imply an unnatural and artificial character.

What to do instead: Use gestures; just don't overdo it. Gestures leave listeners with the perception of confidence, competence and control. But the minute you try to copy a hand gesture, you risk looking contrived.

To know if you are doing any of the above body language mistakes, use a video camera to tape yourself, and play it back while looking at it with a critical eye. Try spotting any annoying gestures you weren't aware of. Now practise growing out of it. Film yourself again, and try to notice improvements.

Chapter 4: YOUR BODY

More than half of all human communication is done non-verbally. Constantly one sends non-verbal messages. When speaking in public, your listeners will judge your message and judge you depending on what they see and what they hear. Learn to use your body to enrich your message.

3.1.- GESTICULATION

When you present a speech, you send two types of messages to your audience. While your voice transmits the verbal message, a large amount of information is transmitted visually by your appearance, your attitude and your physical movements. When you address a group, your listeners will base their opinions of you and your message on what they see as well as on what they hear.

By speaking in public, your body can be an effective tool to bring emphasis and clarity to your words. It is also the most powerful instrument you have to convince an audience of your sincerity, seriousness and enthusiasm. However, if your physical movements distract attention or suggest something that does not agree with your verbal message, your body will defeat your words. If your purpose is to inform, convince, entertain, motivate or inspire, both your body and the personality you project should correspond with your words. To become a successful communicator, you must understand how your body speaks. You can not avoid sending non-verbal messages to your audience, but you can learn to direct and control them. This is one of the purposes of this book, to help you learn to use your whole body as a speech tool.

Would you like for your body to contradict what you say, or do you prefer it to convey the same as your words?

º You can talk about happiness while your body transmits sadness and they will NOT believe you.

º You can talk about motivation while your body transmits discouragement and they will NOT believe you.

º You can try to convince that you are right while your body transmits insecurity and they will NOT believe you.

If you want to convince with a speech, you first have to match your words with your body language.

3.2.- ACTIONS

Actions say more than words, your goal in public speaking is to communicate. To be an effective communicator, you must project seriousness, enthusiasm and sincerity by making your attitude and actions reaffirm your words. If not, the results can be disastrous. Ralph Waldo Emerson once said: "What you are speaks so loudly that it doesn't let me hear what you say." When you speak, people do not judge you only by what you say, they also judge who you are. If the public is not convinced of your sincerity and formality, it is unlikely that they will accept your spoken message. Who you are communicates more clearly through your non-verbal behavior than through your words. When presenting a speech your listeners will use their visual sense to determine if ...

º You are sincere.

º You enjoy the opportunity to address them.

º You truly believe in what you say.

º You feel interest and concern for them.

º You have security and control of the situation.

3.3.- MESSAGE

People get bored with presentations without movement. That is the reason why television news programs always include recordings that show some kind of action. If a fire, a protest or other type of visual activity happens, the news programs will always show it, even if it is not the most important news. A newscast focused on "talking heads" would lose audience, because it could be better heard on the radio.

On the other hand, it is difficult not to look at an object in motion, for example if someone arrives late or the light of a blinking clock tends to divert attention from the speech. People also remember messages that contain different senses. We remember more what we see than what we hear. However, we remember very well when our visual and auditory senses are involved. As a speaker you will have to take advantage of these predispositions by providing visual stimuli that attracts the attention of your audience and improve the retention of your verbal message. Gestures, body movements, facial expressions ... all this can be useful if used skillfully.

3.4.- PUNCTUATION

Punctuation adds meaning, the written language possesses a great variety of symbols for the punctuation of the messages: commas, points, signs of admiration.. among others. But when you speak, you use a totally different set of symbols to show the audience which parts of your speech are more important and to emphasize your words with strength and vitality. Equally effective are gestures, body movements and facial expressions. However, to achieve the greatest possible effect you must coordinate your voice and your body, making them work together. The more communication methods you use, the more effective your communication will be.

3.5.- EXPRESS EFFECTIVELY

How can you put your non-verbal mechanisms in order (posture, gestures, body movements, facial expression and eye contact) and use them effectively when talking? In this section you will learn five general methods to strengthen the verbal image of your body.

Eliminate any movement of distraction "The speaker who stands up and speaks with ease will be heard without discouragement. If your posture and gestures are so elegant and discreet that no one looks at them, then you can be considered a successful speaker. "

When your actions are linked to your words, you will increase the effect of your speech, even if your audience does not notice them consciously. But if your behavior on the podium contains gestures unrelated to your verbal message, those actions will attract attention to those gestures and will be removed from your speech. In fact, instead of adding physical characteristics, sometimes the communicator with initiative should work to get rid of obstacles.

What are these obstacles?

You could probably detect some visual distractions in the presentation of other people by identifying gestures that affect the entire body, such as:

º Wiggling

º Balancing

º Taking small steps

Other obstacles that often affect poorly experienced or inefficient speakers are:

º Grabbing or leaning on the lectern.

º Drum with your fingers.

º Biting or licking lips.

º Clink the coins from the pocket.

º Frown

º Touching hair or clothes.

º Move the head and eyes from side to side like an oscillating fan.

Most of these actions have two things in common: first, they are physical manifestations of nervousness; second, they are performed unconsciously (the speaker does not realize when he performs them). Most of us realize our verbal errors. But unless we have access to video equipment and can record our movements, many of those distracting gestures will remain unchanged.

1.- The first step to eliminate superfluous gestures is to achieve a faithful perception of the verbal image of your body. You can get it if you know which are your most problematic areas and manage to control them in a conscious way in your future presentations. If you find several problem areas, fix them one at a time. When you have eliminated one, go to the next one.

2 .- How to be natural, spontaneous and fluid? The most important rule of all to get your body to speak effectively is *always be you.* The favorite way of speaking today could be described as an "amplified conversation". It is much more informal than the grandiloquent style that characterized the speakers of other times. The emphasis is on communication and sharing ideas, not on acting or sermon. Do not try to imitate other speakers. Instead, react naturally and spontaneously to what you think, feel and say. Strive to have the same authenticity and naturalness that you demonstrate when talking with friends or family.

3.- Let your body reflect your feelings. The "father of modern oratory", Dale Carnegie, wrote: "A person under the influence of his feelings projects his true self, acting naturally and spontaneously. A speaker who shows interest, in general, will be interesting. " If you are interested in a topic, you believe in what you say and you want to share your message with others, the movements of your body should come from within and correspond with what you say. If you get involved in your message, you will be natural and spontaneous without having to consciously think about it.

4.- Strengthen your self-confidence through preparation. Nothing influences a speaker's mental attitude more than knowing he is fully prepared. Knowing this promotes self-confidence, a vital ingredient to speak effectively in public. If you prepare well, your behavior may be externalized to the public instead of internalizing and causing anxiety. You will be less likely to send visual messages that contradict your words and you will discover that it is easier to be natural and spontaneous. Almost effortlessly you will project the magical qualities of sincerity, seriousness and enthusiasm. Practice and rehearse your texts until they are part of you, but do not try to memorize your speech word by word. This can be counterproductive to your preparation as the conscious effort to remember each word will make you nervous and tense. Instead, prepare your texts as well as possible so that you only memorize the flow of ideas. You will see that the words flow spontaneously.

3.6.- POSTURE

The position of your body when speaking communicates by itself its own set of visual messages to the audience. Mainly, it reflects your attitude and transmits it to the listeners by gesturing if you feel security, interest and self-control in yourself and in your way of speaking. A good speaking position offers other advantages to the speaker. It helps you breathe properly and project your voice correctly. It also provides a good starting point from which you can gesticulate and have freedom of movement. By helping you feel alert and comfortable, it reduces nervous tension and minimizes casual and distracting gestures.

EXERCISE:

WHAT IS THE MOST SUITABLE POSTURE TO SPEAK?

Ask someone else to read these two paragraphs aloud and follow the instructions below:

º Stand up straight but not rigid

º Feet separated from 15 to 30 centimeters and with one slightly ahead of the other.

º Balance your weight evenly on the tips of your feet.

º Lean forward a little.

º Your knees should be stretched but not tense.

º Relax the shoulders, but without letting them fall.

º Keep your chest high and flatten your stomach.

º The head should be straight with the chin up, but not uncomfortably.

º Let the arms fall naturally on the sides, with fingers slightly bent.

º Inhale deeply.

Do you feel comfortable? You should adopt an alert but not rigid posture, relaxed but not neglected. If you do not feel it is a natural posture, gently reposition your feet until your body is balanced. Do not keep the same position during a whole presentation. But when moving from one place to another, make sure to balance your body properly.

Chapter 5: Mindset

It all starts with mindset.

Mindset is the reason you are scared of public speaking and believe you may embarrass yourself, forget your train of thought or completely well up.

"When you change the way you look at things, the things you look at change."

When your mindset changes, your actions change and your results change. This first step towards fearlessness deals head on with exactly that - fear.

Just why are we so afraid of public speaking?

Before we get to that, let's understand more about the mind:

Conscious mind / subconscious mind

The conscious mind and the subconscious mind are responsible for what we think we are capable of and what we are afraid of.

- Perception
- Imagination
- Intuition
- Memory
- Reasons
- Experience

These are all the elements that influence the conscious mind.

The subconscious mind internalises what the conscious mind tells it and what is repeated. The conscious mind works on thought and language, the subconscious on emotion - it has no language.

To go from the conscious to the subconscious mind is possible through experiential learning.

Once you walk on hot coals or run a 4-minute mile, the mind internalizes it to the subconscious and whether or not you can do those things becomes a belief.

It's the same for speaking. If you've never spoken before your subconscious belief is that it's scary and difficult as this is your "experience" of it through what you have heard from others.

By speaking even once or twice and making the connections in your mind that you **can** speak publicly (even if you thought it was clunky) begins to create the subconscious belief that public speaking isn't scary or difficult. This belief is strengthened through repetition.

Caveman thinking

The first thing you need to understand is that there are no tigers coming to eat you.

The problem with public speaking and with how our brains are wired, is that the fight or flight response which at one point in our evolution saved us from being eaten, is triggered with the same intensity for situations where we are in much less real danger such as public speaking.

This explains why fear of public speaking and fear of death both rank highly- it's a very similar emotional response, the only difference is that one fear is justified and the other is a misconception.

Exercise

The only way to overcome caveman thinking is to put yourself in "danger". Now, we're not advocating jumping in front of speeding trains, but by challenging yourself and getting your heart racing you can experiment with what it feels like to be terrified for your life... and to survive :-)

Here are some example activities to help:

- Hi-five strangers.
- Start singing aloud in a public space where there is no music.
- Ask people for the time / stop them to ask for directions and keep them holding for as long as possible.

- Keep eye contact with a stranger for longer than normal, if you are asked you can always say you thought they were someone you knew.

- The Selfie challenge. Get as many selfies with strangers as you can.

The principles are to interact with strangers**, to** act without thinking **about it first and to** be in the moment.

You cannot "FAIL" at this. If you approach people and they ignore you, then that is the "worst" outcome, and guess what, you will not die.

Approach people, interact, be ignored, it doesn't matter. The fact you take action and attack your fear is the real success.

Outward focus

One of the fundamental reasons that people are nervous about speaking, is the notion of being judged, of being disliked or "wrong".

The reality is no-one cares about you (sorry!)

No-one cares about you as much as you care about yourself. And it's not as bad as it sounds, it's quite logical. In fact, it's reassuring.

The audience are there to hear what you have to say and interested in what that means for them. Their focus is your talk content, more so than how it's delivered.

When you focus on serving the audience, connecting with them and adding value; you eliminate the fear of freezing up.

When you care less about being judged and care more about delivering a great talk for your audience, you transcend the fear of being judged.

Such outward focus is a cornerstone of becoming a confident speaker.

Exercise

For the next 24 hours, catch yourself saying the words I, me and my. See how often you refer to or talk about yourself and your feelings, thoughts and opinions. You will almost certainly be astonished at how often you talk about yourself (!)

That's ok, we all talk about ourselves, it's human nature.

The exercise here is to shift that focus from "I think this pasta is delicious" to "what do you think about the pasta"

Learning to shift the focus to others and to asking questions about how others feel and what they think is the first step to realising that when you focus on others and on the audience, you can't "fail"

They will forget what you say

This is sad, but true.

A great deal of what you say will be forgotten in the melee of daily life. Your audience will forget most if not all of what you say, but they will not forget how you made them **feel**.

From telling jokes to using emotional content, it's the moments of connection with the audience that are remembered more than what you actually say.

Exercise

Thinking of a time when you felt the emotion you are trying to convey is the best way to relive the emotion and thus transfer it.

If you're talking about love, think of your family, children or significant other.

If you are talking about fear, think about a time when you were afraid and relive the emotion.

Another great example is to say the following words whilst feeling the emotion they represent:happy, bored, sad, angry, bitter, teasing, cynical...

Changing your physiology (your body language and how you speak from tone to tempo and volume) is the best way to connect with the audience.

You cannot transfer what you're not feeling.

Taking this a step further is to relate to the audience. So rather than thinking about a time when you were afraid, you speak about it and connect with the audience by asking questions.

E.g. "I am afraid of spiders. Who here is afraid of spiders by show of hands?"

Reach one person

We've established that your talk is not about you - it's about the audience. But the reality is that you will not connect with every member of the audience - and nor should you.

By focussing on connecting with and delivering value to only one audience member you not only reduce the pressure upon yourself to please everyone. You also make your delivery more personable and relatable as this shift in focus alters your deliver.

Example

When you speak, imagine there is a person in the audience who has flown in especially to hear you.

They recognise you as the expert on your chosen topic and have waited months for that moment.

Speak to that person.

Speak with that person in mind, you are going to change their life and add value to them through your speaking, you can't let anything stand in your way as you don't want to let this person down.

You owe it to them to deliver the best talk you can.

You can't transfer what you're not feeling

When it comes to focussing on your audience and serving them, emotion and connection are vitally important.

Without connection, your content loses the majority of its impact and it's clear to the audience when you as a speaker aren't connected to what you are saying.

When you understand that you can't transfer feelings you're not feeling yourself. Everything will change for your speaking style and delivery.

Exercise

Think of a holiday location you went to and didn't like or enjoy.

In the mirror, recorded on your phone or to a friend or family member, say a few improvised words about how much you like that holiday destination and how great it is.

Now think of the most awesome and enjoyable holiday destination you've ever been to.

In the mirror, recorded on your phone or to a friend or family member, say a few improvised words about how much you like that holiday destination and how great it is.

Notice the difference in your tonality, your body language and the length of what you have to say. The topic you connect to more will be obvious.

There is no perfect.

When you plan a talk, you have an idea of how perfect it should be. Perfect length, perfect delivery, perfect content and great audience reaction. And why not? We all want to do our best.

The reality is there is no perfect. The pressure to achieve perfection can be a leading cause of stumbling and losing your train of thought. If you accept that the delivery you give is the best you will achieve, then the pressure lessens.

If you miss something or jumble the order of your talk, most of the time the audience won't know - only you know how your talk should be.

If you connect with the audience, add value and create rapport - THAT is perfection.

Exercise

To realise that perfection is an illusion, you need to deliberately act imperfectly and experience first-hand that life moves on.

This is like the caveman thinking exercise. Your expectations and thoughts can limit you when in reality so much more is possible.

There is one awesome activity for this

- Approach someone in the street as though you know them. Say "hi <name> I haven't seen you in ages!" and as they say hello, realise you don't know them, apologize and move on.

This activity starts with your image of speaking with the person as though you know them. Visualise them as the actual person. As you approach and establish you don't know them, you actively destroy the perfect visualisation you had in your mind.

Kaizen

Kaizen is the Japanese word for continual improvement.

Speaking, like everything in life, evolves over time and as you speak more, so your ability to speak and your technique and ability improves.

When you understand the first few times you speak you will make "mistakes" and will spot things to improve, you also understand that by trusting the process, you will improve over time.

No speaker ever began perfectly, it's a learning curve.

Repeatedly using the exercises here and taking every speaking opportunity you can is the route to being the best speaker you can be.

Chapter 6: NLP Techniques Can Help You Overcome Your Public Speaking Fear

What is NLP or neuro-linguistic programming? It's behavioral technology that has a set of rules, attitudes and methods regarding real-life behavior.

NLP lets you change, take on or get rid of behaviors you see fit and enables you to pick how you want to feel mentally, emotionally and physically.

NLP is only a theory, but it may work on the subconscious mind. NLP isn't like other methods – it's a learned process. You don't have to understand medicine or psychology.

The NLP states the mind is similar to a computer with different programs running. While most are unconscious, it can show people techniques to overcome them (if so desired).

What are the processes? The mind works with three senses (even though humans have five):

Visual (Seeing)

Auditory (Hearing)

Kinesthetic (Feelings)

Everybody uses one of them during processes.

Some people see the word using their eyes. Other people are considered auditory, using their ears to hear things. And, then there are others who are kinesthetic, using their feelings to go through life.

For visual people, the world is seen through the eyes, which means the visual process can cause the fear of public speaking.

For instance, a person with a genuine public speaking fear may experience shaky hands, cracked voice, rapid heartbeat and more. For these people, it could be the fear of a bad speech that causes them to feel this way.

Visually, they see people laughing at them while they can't remember what they're supposed to talk about. They're unable to control these images and get rid of them.

What is happening to visual people? The mind is playing a movie in its head — something scary and unable to get away from. It's similar to when you actually watch a scary movie — you're afraid and want to get away, but it's just a movie.

For these individuals, the fear is caused by the pictures in their head. The subconscious mind reacts as if you're watching a movie (but this movie is your life).

Traditional psychology wants to find the root cause for the fear. It looks at the past to see what has affected the future.

The NLP, on the other hand, is a short treatment and doesn't look at the past since the root cause may be something that happened long before you were born.

How can people deal with their fear then?

Visual Individuals

Are you a visual person? If so, then chances are some pictures are in your head. It's important to understand what you're seeing. Are they?

In black and white or colors?

Smooth or rough?

Moving quickly or slowly?

In details?

In first or third position?

For a person who is visual, they can see images of people laughing at them or making a mistake, which led to being embarrassed. To get over this, it's important to understand what it is they see.

This means having them describe it in great detail – from their eyes. What is it do they see happening?

When these images play over and over, the mind generates a response (fear). A person knows it's all in their mind, but the effect is still the same.

The premise behind the NLP is that you cannot fight thoughts. You can't just tell yourself that you're not afraid because the mind doesn't accept that. Your mind continues to play the images over and over.

What needs to happen then is to make changes – adding in effects, changing angles, etc. While this sounds like an impossibility, it's not!

For a person who sees things in black and white and from first position, they need to move their thoughts to third position and in color. Stand at the sidelines to watch yourself giving the speech.

The idea is to see yourself there in the crowd as well as the crowd itself. Ensure that the images allowed you to start seeing yourself from a distance — further and further. The idea is not to see the details as clearly.

Rather than fight the movie, you can manipulate it. The movie and images are not so scary anymore!

When you must do a public speech, you can use the process to help you overcome the fear. Before you know it, you won't have to do it all. The fear will be pretty much gone. When you speak, you can focus on the message and not the fear.

The NLP gives visual individuals a quick solution to reduce or eliminate the fear —

changing it from an up-close problem to something that's in the distance.

Auditory Individuals

What about people who are auditory? What can be done to help them alleviate their fear? The goal is to diminish the power of the auditory process that generates fear.

This is usually a voice or sound. For instance, you could be telling yourself that people will laugh at you or that you can't do something. You may even hear people laughing at you.

While it's not possible to make a sound smaller like you can if it's a visual process, it can still be weakened. There are several options, however, the biggest one is to create differences in the voice.

Rather than hearing it normally, consider making it sound funny – a childish-like voice or something in a chipmunk's voice.

The idea is to change the voice so that it's no longer scary. In fact, you could find yourself laughing at the voice.

Understanding the NLP

These are just some ways in which you can use NLP to get past your fear and do what you need to do. There are other techniques you can do such as adding in background music, effects and more to overcome the issues that generate the fear you have.

You can use to improve various skills such as:

Better communicator

More income

Increased efficiency

Simply put, it's a set of methods and techniques that can help you improve your life and give you better control over your mind. Would that not be something you would like forward to? You would have control over your mind; not your mind controlling you.

Since this is about public speaking, it simply means the NLP allows you to create a message that's clearer and more concise to the individuals it's being given to.

The NLP was only created in the last few years and is still undergoing development. It would do you a wonder of good to learn what you can. Be sure to do some research and see how you can apply the NLP to your life.

Your Belief System Can Create Fear

Many times, fear is caused by a belief system. How is that? A belief is more powerful than knowledge. How you see the world is based on the belief system.

Belief isn't something that can be proven – many times. For instance, the belief in God cannot be proven, but nearly all beliefs in life are not regarded as being absolute.

Certain believes cannot be proven true or false, but they can still benefit you – to help you to attain goals.

When you consider the fear of public speaking, you may have a few beliefs causing that fear. Studies show that the most common belief causing fear is limiting belief, which is that it is normal to be fearful or have anxiety when speaking publicly.

Do you have to accept this belief that it's normal to be fearful? Do you feel it's okay to have that fear of speaking in public?

Probably so!

Why is that? It's usually the result of what you have experienced and what society has taught you.

Of course, one has to wonder if it's normal to be scared of something. After all, if it's just a belief, is it really normal? The belief that causes your fear is the result of you accepting the fact that you have it and will experience it.

Empower yourself by changing your belief. Realize that there is nothing normal about being afraid, especially about being afraid to speak in public. Realize the fear is irrational and it's not normal.

Remind yourself that public speaking doesn't have to be a scary thing, but something you can feel relaxed about.

Do you see how making changes to your belief system will change how you move through life – how you see it and respond?

Rather than believing in something that makes you afraid, why not change it into something powerful and positive?

Think about the belief. There are millions of people who have no public speaking fear at all. In fact, they relish in the task. The idea is to choose what you have a belief in. Why not empower yourself?

What Kinds Of Beliefs Can You Do Without?

There are several types of beliefs you need to eliminate from your mindset:

"It's okay that you're nervous." — Why is that? Shouldn't you want to relax? That belief is very limiting.

"You're either born to speak in public or not." — Not even, but it's this belief that hinders you from being successful when talking publicly. You can learn how to become a successful public speaker — in due time.

The only person stopping you from being successful is yourself. And, regardless of what you may think, nobody is born to be a natural public speaker.

"You can't overcome public speaking fear." — Don't you believe that for even a minute. Millions of people have been able to get over their fear of public speaking.

"The audience would like to see you fail." – The majority of people in your audience have been in your shoes, and they actually admire you for having the guts and courage to get up on stage and talk.

If they came to hear you talk about a subject, they do not want you to fail.

Create a belief system so that you can succeed in your quest for whatever you are going after. The power is in your hands to believe what you want to believe in.

Chapter 7: How to Overcome Stage Fright

If you're reading a book about public speaking, I'm going to assume you probably suffer from stage fright. It's not an uncommon occurrence, and many professional public speakers have admitted having stage fright over the years. If they can get up on a stage almost every day and make a living at giving speeches, despite suffering from stage fright, then you can move past it, too. I'm not going to say it is going to go away. It's more about changing your outlook and recognizing what is happening. Then you can move past it, but you might always have a little twinge before you go onstage to speak.

Remember Who Is Performing

Remember the audience is there to see you and hear you. It's your expertise, your gift to them, and your unique ability to get them out of their house and to their seat as your audience member. Of all the people in that room, you're the one who knows more about what is going to be said and who is going to be performing than anyone else there. Let yourself be the master of that moment.

Forget the Stakes

You heard me. Forget about who's in front of you for the time being. You've thought about that enough as you prepared, so take a good look at the people who are going to be listening to you and realize they are just like you. And you know what? They don't matter. You're the one performing.

Performance over the Audience

What you're delivering is actually more important than who you're delivering it to. Yes, the audience matters, but you've already factored that in. When it comes time to deliver the speech, you are the one who matters at that moment.

Maintain your focus on your performing and not your audience. You should have practiced enough with a fake audience to know if they will like the jokes or not.

Be a Broadcaster

Radio and television are great proving grounds for actors and on stage performers because they allow you to practice without the physical distraction of having a visible audience. It sounds simplistic, but get some time with a camera and a microphone in order to focus more on the performance than the audience. Remember to practice so you can review yourself later and critique your movements.

Practice Like You Mean It

The worst mistake performers make is they do not feel the weight of the performance before they actually deliver it. If you don't perform at your full volume, pitch, and cadence, your body and mind are not going to know what it's going to be like and have the chance to adapt. So replicate your performance as much as you can before you actually do it.

Visualize Mistakes

There's always that moment when you realize you made a mistake onstage, so what are you going to do about it? It's best to visualize those mistakes before they ever happen so you can have a game plan. If they don't occur, great, if they do, no big deal; you have a plan for what you're going to do no matter what. If your worst fear is you're going to sneeze during your presentation, think about what you'll say and how you'll move on. If it's you'll show up with no pants on, then think about your preparation before the speech and how you can avoid that error.

Slow Down

When someone is nervous, they tend to speed up their speech so much the audience cannot keep up. This increases the likelihood of slipping up and saying something embarrassing or detrimental to the speech, so slow down. Use a metronome during rehearsal to control the speed at which you're talking. This forces your brain to get into a workable pace.

Buffer Your Performance

Arrive where you're going to speak early, and arrive alone or with a few supporters who understand you need some space. Settle in and disconnect from everyone around you. Turn the smartphone off. Use this time to review lines and notes, and have a beverage that's non-alcoholic and non-caffeinated to get in the mood. Over time, you'll have personal rituals that will help you get into the mindset of what you're about to do and what you want to achieve.

We'll talk more about how to take control of your thoughts and emotions before you get onstage and when you're actually on stage in chapter six. First, let's talk more about your body language.

Chapter 8: Actions Speak As Loud As Your Words

Now that you know what you are going to talk about, go ahead and familiarize yourself with your audience and the manner in which you're going to deliver your speech. After preparing for the day of reckoning, it's finally time to bring it on. You are now ready to deliver your speech with ease and style.

The moment you walk into the room marks the official beginning of your speech. The way you walk and present yourself will be like the first words out of your mouth. This is why you should remember a few things about what to observe as you deliver your speech.

Posture

Slouching in front of your audience is not the good way to start your presentation.

Unless you are a ninety-year-old woman with osteoporosis, you have no excuse when it comes to maintaining the correct posture. Remember that your physical appearance is part of the armor that will lead you to win this word battle. Go on the stage or stand in front of your boss with loose muscles and drooping shoulders and your audience will think you'd rather be in bed. On the other hand, keeping your muscles too tense will make your actions jerky and will again make your audience think that you would rather be anywhere other than there. Yes, it may be true that you want to be sipping a cup of good coffee in your bed instead of getting your heart worked over by talking in public, but you have no choice.

The key here is, if you want your listeners to feel comfortable watching and hearing you speak, you must also project a vibe that you are comfortable with what you are doing. Maintain an upright posture and relax. Don't grip your notes as if your life depends on them.

Body Placement

You may consider a podium your new best friend and cling to it like an old lover. But, when used excessively, it can serve as a barricade between you and your audience, hindering the establishment of a much needed connection. It is advisable to step away from the podium from time to time to avoid making your listeners think you are afraid of them. Keeping close to your listeners is a sign of trust and will send the message that you are open to the experience.

Body movement

When you are speaking, moving around is recommended for a lot of reasons. Unless you really have to stand behind a podium because of an immovable microphone, don't stand in one place too long during the speech. Move from time to time to provide your audience something new to look at. However, don't make your movement resemble pacing. You are not an expectant father in a hospital waiting for your baby so don't even think about it.

Moreover, you should maintain an erect posture in order to facilitate your speech. Standing straight helps in comfortable breathing and preventing fatigue. It also lets you initiate eye contact with your listeners easily and project your voice better. The psychological effect of standing straight is the perception that you are confident in your own skin and you're well-prepared.

Included in body movements are the gestures that you should or shouldn't do. If you are used to flailing your arms around like a fish out of the water when you are speaking, get out of the delusion that you *are* a fish during formal public speaking events. Gestures should skate the line between being overdramatic and subdued. Both extremes wouldn't help push your message. On the one hand, using huge gestures is sure to distract your audience and will affect your credibility. On the other hand, refusing to use any gesture at all robs you of chances to emphasize your points, and express enthusiasm.

Facial Expression

Facial expressions can be used at will for your advantage, but if not controlled accordingly could be detrimental to you as a speaker. People are great observers of expressions and a disturbance is created if there's a conflict between what people see on your face and what they hear from your mouth.

The eyes are the most vital element of facial expressiveness. This is why eye contact is a topic that must be separately and thoroughly discussed.

The facial expression that you must display should fit the message you are conveying. You can't smile when you are talking about death or something serious. Avoid wearing an expressionless face for it would signify that you are either afraid or indifferent.

The rule is simple: let your message show in your face.

Dress

How other people will perceive you can be affected by the way you dress. If you dress inappropriately, your credibility will be doubted by your audience. Make it a point to match your look with the type of speaking business you are in. If it's just a casual speaking event, you can opt for jeans and a T-shirt. Business presentations would require you to don suits, dresses, ties, shoes, etc. Really formal ones could mean wearing formal gowns or tuxedoes.

Girls, be careful with the accessories that you wear as well. Some of them could make for very distracting materials for your audience and they'll end up watching the way your bracelets jingle instead of paying attention to you.

Chapter 9: How To Wow Your Audience

In addition to polishing your public speaking skills, you also need to focus on wooing your audience, so they become your loyal listeners. Here are some workable tips you can use to woo an audience and turn them into fans.

Become a storyteller

Audiences don't appreciate speakers who keep blabbering facts, figures, and complicated pieces of information. Audiences come to hear you tell something amazing and inspiring. This is where storytelling comes in.

To inspire your audience, become a storyteller. Turn your life experiences and that of your loved ones into exciting stories, tell them passionately to your audience, and see how quickly they become engrossed in your speech. Also, add the elements of humor, emotion, and adventure to your stories to make them entertaining, spicy, inspiring, and exciting.

Tell a Unique Fact

Make sure to include an interesting, but unique piece of information into your speech. This excites the audience and makes them feel that you elaborately researched the topic to make it different from what's already available.

Focus on benefitting the audience and not selling your product/ service

If you are selling a product or service via speech, try not to make a promotional and marketing speech. Rather, your focus should be on how your audience will benefit from that product. Your audience should feel that you care enough about them to dig out a useful product, so they become interested in making a purchase from you.

End your speech five minutes early

Make sure to run short. If you have an hour to give your speech, end it in 55 minutes. Ending your speech a little early makes your audience feel that you respect their time and the fact they have come all the way to listen to you. It also prevents your speech from becoming a drag.

Give them something to think about and do

Inspiring your audience is important. However, you also need to give your audience something to ponder on, and something to do so they can apply the knowledge gained from your speech.

For instance, if you are motivating them to follow their dreams, you must give actionable tips at the end of the speech so that your audience actually pursue their goals. If you are inspiring them to become great leaders, make sure to tell them how to accomplish that goal. When you help your audience achieve their goals, they start valuing you.

Ask for input

Do ask your audience to share their opinions, suggestions, and input with you during, or at the end of the speech. This makes them feel that you value their ideas, and are welcoming them to participate in your speech. Plus, this makes the session interactive and entertaining.

The trick to making these tips work is actually trying them out. Implement these strategies and all the information you have learnt from this public speaking workbook and easily objectify your goal of becoming an excellent professional public speaker.

CHAPTER *10*: The Heart Of The Mind:

MEMORY DEVELOPMENT

' Memory is a way of holding onto the things you love, the things you are, the

things you never want to lose.'

– Edward de Bono

Memory development begins at a very tender stage in life, as

we are going to find out in this chapter.

I became conscious of my strong memory when I first delivered

that story to my nursery school kids for almost 20 minutes.

My turning point in memory development came when I was a

teenager in high school. One renowned Nigerian preacher by the name of George Adegboyi came to the city of Mombasa to speak

in a church; he is famous for his way of speaking and ability to

quote scriptures from memory. He could quote over four hundred

bible scriptures in one sermon. I got very intrigued by this so I

got a hold of his tapes and listened to them and asked myself,

what does this man have?

I came to the conclusion that I needed to test my mind and

see whether it was made of the same ingredients as this man.

Immediately, I dedicated myself to the study and memorizing of

scriptures, a fit I had been introduced to when I was in Sunday school to recite to them before the adult congregation in church.

After deliberately investing myself into this exercise, I soon got a chance to speak at a church congregation. I was amazed that in a thirty minutes sermon I was able to quote off memory ten passages of scriptures. This was no mean task for a seventeen year old and to the great inspiration of the congregation. I have since continued to use this skill of memorization as a premium aspect of my public speaking.

The interest to build a strong memory in the area of speaking was so strong that I ended up spending so much time trying to memorize quotes and scriptures whether I had a speaking

engagement or not. Soon it began to pay up for me. I remember

the first speech I delivered when I was in bible school, I quoted

from the Heart

over fifteen scriptures within fifteen minutes and since then for a

very long time it has become my way of speaking.

Once I had been invited to address the Christian Union

students of Catholic University of Eastern Africa, and for twenty

Public Speaking

minutes of my address I quoted over thirty five scriptures. Quoting

- memorized scriptures became part of me, my mind was thinking in terms of what I had impressed in there. I remember one day

when I spoke at the Redeemed Gospel Church in Kawangware,

on the outskirts of Nairobi City, I was only twenty three years of

age. I quoted over seventy scriptures within that sermon which

lasted for around forty minutes. The associate pastor when

commenting about my sermon acknowledged that was the third

walking bible he had encountered in his life.

To me memorizing of scriptures, quotes and phrases was not

just for the sake of it, but to prove whether this mind is strong and can process and store information for use in the future. I was

actually a curious student of the mind, something which later

provoked me to enroll and study psychology so that I may be able

to understand the human mind very well.

I was twenty-four years of age, I had been sent by the non-

denominational organization I was working with to represent

them as a key speaker in a Christian Union rally at Mutomo

girls, a school in the southern part of Kitui District. I vividly

remember it had been along stretch of speaking engagements.

For three weeks I was out of Mombasa, I had gone to Kisumu

for a conference and speaking engagements, and then I came

to Nairobi where I was speaking at the Catholic University

Christian Union and then I was in Mutomo Girls. The meeting

was full packed to overflowing with over one thousand students

and teachers from different secondary schools across the district.

In my sermon which was branded "holiness" I quoted over ninety

scriptures off head in forty five minutes, such was my growth in

memory development.

What Is Memory Development?

Memory is the ability to remember the things we have experienced,

imagined and learned. There is no way memory can work without taking information in, store it in some manner so that you may be able to retrieve it later. You can never be able to deliver speeches extemporaneously unless first, you develop your memory in such a manner that you can internalize speeches and deliver them from the heart.

Richard Shiffrin and Richard Atkinson (1969) developed an influential memory model which assumes that memory involves the processing of information in three successive stages: sensory memory, short term memory and long term memory. Sensory memory lasts for a brief period, from less than one second to several seconds. When you attend to information in sensory

memory, it is transferred to short term memory which stores

information for up to about twenty seconds unless you maintain

it through a mental rehearsal. If you do not attend to it, you

lose the information. The short term memory is also known as

the working memory because it processes information, sieves it

and pushes it to the long term memory which is able to store

information for up to a lifetime.

from the Heart

The handling of information at each memory stage has been

compared to information processing by a computer, which

involves encoding, storage and retrieval.

I want to draw your attention to the type of long term memory

Public Speaking

- known as explicit memory or declarative memory. Explicit

memory involves the conscious recollection of information, such

Dan Mugera

as specific facts or events, especially in humans, information that

can be verbally communicated for example, recounting the events

of a movie, story or describing a basic principle of something you

learned.

To my understanding explicit memory is the one used by

speakers to enable them to speak from the heart. Why so? Because it involves the conscious recollection of information that can be

verbally communicated. You verbally communicate information

when you are speaking. Tulvin (1993) subdivides explicit memory

into semantic memory, which is a person's knowledge about the

world which includes fields of expertise, general knowledge and

everyday knowledge of words, people, places and common things.

Episodic memory includes memories of personal experience tied

to particular times and places. For example, can you remember

on 31st of December 1999 where you were and what you were

doing?

Joseph Murphy, the author of The Power of the Subconscious *Mind*, in paraphrasing his words wrote that, we think with our conscious mind and what we habitually think sinks into our subconscious mind which creates according to the nature of our thoughts. The subconscious mind is the seat of memory, thoughts and habits. Therefore it is important to know that if you want to internalize speeches, you definitely need to be aware of how your mind works. This leads us to another subtopic of how to memorize speeches.

The Possibility to Memorize Speeches

Delivering a speech extemporaneously to Kenya Commercial Bank staff at Kencom House in (2012) led one senior manager after the

speech to approach me and asked curiously, "You delivered all

that without notes". You could clearly see the shock in his eyes. I

can remember in 2010 December, I spoke to a group of youths at

the Word of Life Centre in Diani and after the speech one young

lady approached me and asked, "You mean you were not reading

from any where?" and my answer was, "I do not read my speeches

I speak because public reading is not public speaking."

This is to affirm that it is possible to speak from the heart.

I simply seek to build your faith into this arena of possibility thinking that you as an individual can and if you can, as my

good friend Joseph Obwanda the author of *Become Your Excellency*

usually says, "Then you must".

Memorizing of speeches can take a great deal of efforts, but

it is far much better than standing before an audience trying to

give a speech that you do not remember. This can affect your

credibility and destroy your rapport and even yourself esteem.

Principles of Memorizing

from the Heart

In memorizing of speeches, you simply need to understand a few

key principles. These are:

1. Existing cognitive structures

2. Interest

Public Speaking

• 3. Spaced repetition

Dan Mugera

Existing cognitive structure

It is important to note that most people work against their

own memory. We can only remember things better if we can

relate them with something that we already know. Connection

of information goes a long way in enabling you remember things.

So what is your existing cognitive structure?

Interest

If you are interested in something you are more likely to

remember it than a person who is not interested in it. I remember

what I learnt in 1998 that "character is the belief in an absolute

system of rights and wrongs combined with the will to do what

is right regardless of the personal cost." I have not forgotten that,

why? Because I was interested in the information.

Spaced repetition

When you learn something, it passes through short term

memory then it is passed into long term memory. Spaced

repetition is the secret of moving information from short term

memory into the permanent long term memory. That is you

repeat the information you have learnt, give it space and repeat it

again. Continue with this process for several hours and days and

you will be able to remember information like the back of your

hands.

Steps to Speech memorization

• First, make a very general and broad outline of your speech.

• Memorize it by using repetition technique. After memorizing

it, fill in some details. Memorize them the next day. Then fill in

even more details, and memorize them.

• Begin slowly integrating full sentences, stories and major

points. You can go from the broad outline to the text of your speech. The outline will be the easiest to remember, and it will

provide the "memory tree" to hang the rest of your speech on.

By the time you finish, you will have familiarised yourself with

the speech.

• If you are still having a hard time memorizing your speech, spice

up the environment you are in. Do not make it distracting, you

can not try to memorize a speech and at the same time you are

watching television and the radio is on. Walk around while

you memorize. This will help your mind relax and focus on the

speech. On your off time, find new, interesting things that are pertinent to your topic. It could be a story which you will hear, a quote shared by a friend or a statistic you read on the newspaper.

- Once you memorize the outline, returning to it the next day and adding more text will serve to cement it in your memory. Once you have something memorized, review it a day or two later.

from the Heart

After that, review it in a week if you have more time. If you still remember it, review it once more and it will be unforgetable.

- You can also make use of mnemonics (memory aiding devices) like the method of loci (location), key word method and

Public Speaking

PQ4R'S method. In the method of loci, one stores information

- in imaginative locations like in rooms or office draws so you can retrieve them later. In key word method, you can form an acronym out of a word and fill the anecdotes which will make it easier to remember.

For example wisdom to remember that;

*W*ise

*I*nspired

*S*ervants

*D*edicate

*O*pportunities

*M*eaningfully

PQ4R'S method is an acronym which stands for;

*P*review, *Q*uestion, *R*ead, *R*eflect, *R*ecite, and *R*eview.

This will help you to organize information, ask questions, reflect

and think about it and review it. This will make retrieval and

encoding of information effective.

It is noteworthy that you can use this process to memorize a

speech in a month's time, two week's time, one week's time or

even when you have just a few days. The only difference will come

if you have just some few minutes to memorize a speech then the

only thing which will count is existing cognitive structure.

How to improve your memory

There are indeed several ways which can help you improve your

memory, but for the purpose of our learning allow me to discuss

three practical ways which I believe will be of benefit to any

person.

1. Good rest.

This will enable your brain to function at maximum capacity.

For you to attain good rest, you need to regularly sleep for six to

eight hours daily. We are leaving in a busy world today and if you

are not carefully you will realize you do not rest at all.

Majority of the people have woken up to discover they are

workaholics with no time to rest, they leave the house very early in the morning and come back nearly midnight, go to sleep and

wake up at 4am for seven days in a week. At the same time you

may realize you do not have time to unwind or even to exercise.

Soon you might get burnout which comes with extreme fatigue

and stress. All this will tamper with your mind and it could be

hard for it to function at maximum level.

2. Good nourishment.

You need to eat a well balanced diet which will enable

your body pH to be balanced. Your normal body pH needs to

be 7.3%. If it goes up above 8.2% or lower than 6.8%, then you

could be vulnerable to diseases and sicknesses. Your body needs to consume 80% alkaline foods and 20% acidic foods in a day.

Most of the time we do it vice versa, we take a lot of acidic food

from the Heart

stuffs and drinks and wonder why we wake up in the morning

feeling tired and not in a position to memorize information

easily. Nutritionists categorize some foods as good for increasing

memory ability. Some of these foods are; fish, nuts like almonds,

Public Speaking

ground nuts, and rosemary leaves.

• Dan Mugera

You must be watchful of what you allow your mind to

consume; good nourishment to me is not only about the body but also your mental health. Recognize the fact that memory is part

of the mind and you must do everything in your power to make

sure you enrich your mind with good stuff.

3. Free your mind from altering substances

Mind altering substances like alcohol and drugs will not help

you to improve your memory. Remember memory development

takes time and you will need to invest the necessary time so

that you can improve your memory. It is the active decision to

get better and the number of hours you push yourself to improve

that will make the difference. This will demand focus and a sober

mind to achieve the highest results.

Chapter 11: Becoming the Best Speaker

There are some speakers who, despite their well-written notecards, or their perfectly timed speeches, are unable to get the attention of their audience. These speakers are usually lacking in experience or confidence, or in the worst cases, they are lacking in both those important aspects. This chapter will focus on how you can deliver a good speech, use gestures to your advantage and rid yourself of stage fright.

Dressed for Success

Once you have your speech written, you need to dress appropriately for the occasion. A public speaker is judged by his or her audience the minute he or she steps into the room. As a speaker, you are responsible for the way you look, move and speak. How you dress is important, as your choice in clothing says a lot about how you see yourself, and how you want to be seen.

Check the attire required for the event, and be sure to plan your outfit a few days before you deliver your speech. Male speakers should look clean, composed and decent. No one appreciates a kill joy or a sore thumb when it comes to formal or semi-formal events. If you know that the event you will be speaking at requires a coat and tie, then exert extra effort to find clothes that suit you, as well as the event.

However, be sure that you can easily and comfortably move in whatever clothes you choose. If you look good but are unable to deliver your speech to the best of your ability because your pants or shirt is too tight, then you will have defeated the purpose of looking your best.

Female speakers should know what kind and how much makeup are needed for each event. You want to look your best in front of the public. Dressing well is a means of boosting your confidence. You might not believe it at first, but being able to stand on appropriate heels, and face your audience with your hair and face perfectly styled does affect how you speak. Choose clothes that will make you feel beautiful and in control of the situation to help you speak with grace and authority.

Don't be a robot!

One trait common to most novice public speakers is the use of robot-like movements and gestures. Worse still is the absence of any gesture or movement at all. Some speakers become so focused on what they are saying that they forget to engage the audience with their hands, eyes and movements. Good speakers know that it is important to use their body when speaking in front of a group.

Remember that your voice is not the only part of your body capable of communicating. Your eyes can convey excitement, fear, passion and joy. Your hands can draw and sustain the attention of the crowd, can create rhythm and images for your audience. Your movements tell your listeners to watch you, to listen to you with rapt attention.

Don't be a robot! Move as you speak. Move closer to your audience during the crucial parts of your speech. Use your hands and your face to share your emotions with the crowd. Maximize the space given to you. Let your audience feel that they are part of your speech. Don't be stoic or monotonous. Feel the emotions in your speech as passionately as when you first wrote your thoughts on paper, and then share that passion with your audience.

Practice for confidence, practice for perfection.

The key to ridding yourself of stage fright or speech anxiety is to keep practicing. If you know that your speech will be strictly timed, then practice with a timer near you. If you know that you are not that confident when it comes to speaking in front, then practice as much as you can! The more you practice delivering your speech, the more comfortable you will be. The more comfortable you are, the higher your confidence; and the higher your confidence, the better your speech delivery.

Practice delivering your speech in front of your friends. Let them hear what you have to say so they can tell you which aspects you can improve on, and which points are your strongest. This will also teach you the humility and open-mindedness that are crucial to your development as a public speaker.

If you have friends or acquaintances that are used to public speaking, then have them go over your speech with you. Listen to their advice, and apply those you deem fit. Remember that this is your speech, and at the end of the day, the audience will want to listen to your thoughts, your opinions, and your ideas.

Chapter 12: Audience Tools - How to Use Voice Tone and Pause

The speaker needs to know what means of influence on the audience he has. This is a whole complex:

a) speech (power, pitch, and sound level; intonation; timbre and melody of speech; pause (logical and psychological))

b) verbal (word)

c) non-verbal (gesture, facial expression, pose, look)

Reception "initial pause" - its role is psychological. This is needed in order to collect the attention of the audience, to give her time to consider the speaker, and the opportunity to prepare for the perception of speech. During the initial pause, the speaker calms down, relieves excitement, focuses. You can intrigue the listener with a pause, and by its absence, you can be overwhelmed, and in both cases, it is a psychological device with which attention is drawn, and interest is aroused.

Attention, according to figurative expression, "the door to the human mind," is held by special techniques: compositional, speech, and methodological. Compositional means of enhancing attention and interest include an intriguing beginning, intermittent (dotted) deployment of the thesis, question-answer course of reasoning, contrasting comparison of arguments, and an expressive conclusion.

Speech means are the use of literary images, quotes, the use of different styles, expressive vocabulary; the artistry of presentation; dramatization of speech; intonational expressiveness - varying the strength, pitch, pace of speech, psychological breaks.

Methodological tools include consideration of problem situations, highlighting the main points of the speech, polemic nature of the presentation, eye contact with the audience, use of visibility and technical means, use of appeals to the audience to renew attention.

Persuade with Your Energy and Your Charisma - Non-Verbal Tools of Audience Captivation

I strongly suggest adopting non-verbal ways of influencing the audience through gestures and eyes.

If you want to establish mutual understanding and confidential contact with people, be absolutely open. Do not sit or stand in front of them with your legs crossed and arms folded across the chests or locked in a lock. Also, exclude the foot-on-foot pose. All these poses are closed; they do not give free flow of energy between the speaker and the listeners. On the contrary, remove all the clamps, and keep your hands with your open palm towards the listener, slightly spreading your fingers (about five millimeters apart). At a non-verbal level, this sends information, "I am open, ready for cooperation, and trust you." In this situation, only a gentle presentation of information and calm convincing speech are necessary. The emerging trust does not oblige a person to act in accordance with your preferences, he has a choice, and therefore, the ability to be himself and act consciously.

How to influence the listener if it is necessary to convey a thought prompting action? For example, your company needs to increase production. Confidently speaking about the difficulties, gaining understanding from people, use a different gesture.

First, a hand with slightly spread fingers (1-2 cm) is located at the level of the solar plexus, palm down. It is as if you are brushing the space below it. Then, at the moment when you pronounce the main, persuading, or inviting phrases, you make an additional message of energy with your hand.

Hold your palm relaxed, turn your palm over smoothly and flexibly, and then give your fingers and palms stiffness. Such a gesture prompts you to act, and people will hear you and feel the need to obey your requirements.

Emphasis: despite the fact that the message is solid, it still comes from the heart, and therefore people will hear what you want to convey to them.

If you need to enhance the effect, then the gesture is performed with two hands at the same time. Well, these gestures bring the greatest effect if, when doing them, standing in a position of strength - it subjugates.

If, in this situation, it is necessary that people act in accordance with your will, and at the same time, you want to be slightly democratic, then you need to soften this gesture. At that moment, when the palm is directed towards the audience, the fingers do not close, but, on the contrary, are parted about two centimeters apart, and the palm is held firmly, but not rigidly.

In the first case, you insist that people submit to your choice and your will, in the second, you gently show your will, and still leave the right to choose the person. The first gesture is acceptable when the situation is extreme, an emergency when time is short, and you need to think and act quickly when the leader needs to take responsibility, and unconditional submission to the team is required. The second gesture is acceptable in an extraordinary situation but requiring a conscious quick decision.

- If you need to convey to your interlocutor a thought, as they say, "drive" it into your head, you need to hold your palm firmly, connecting all your fingers together. And during the conversation, gesturing, point the palm of your hand toward the listener at the level of the solar plexus. The palm can be held either perpendicularly or parallel to the floor. You can also fold your arms in a prayer gesture in front of your chest, and during the process of making a speech, point them with your fingertips to the listener at the level of the heart. Note, however. It cannot be directed to the head level. Let me explain why.

When we point our palm at the level of the solar plexus, we simply give the listener the resource necessary for him to make a decision. To make any decision, a person needs energy, and if it is not enough, then, with the help of these gestures, the speaker transmits it. At the solar plexus level, we add decisiveness. And when we direct our palms folded in a prayer gesture to the level of the person's heart, we simply direct the energy, thanks to which our information, figuratively speaking, can reach the person's heart, we will touch upon him the feelings that will help him to make the necessary decision. Both the first and second options are safe for both the speaker and the listener because it is just about transferring the resource. And if you direct your palms to the level of the head, then this will mean only one thing - suppressing the will of the listener, and this is fraught with negative consequences. We have no right to manipulate people!

If we need to calm a noisy audience, we need to keep our eyes above the heads of the audience, not fixing ourselves on individual faces, press our elbows to the sides of the body, raise our palms with rigidly folded fingers to shoulder level (it looks like a gesture "give up", only palms are not above the head, and at shoulder level). Then slowly lower your hands, palm down. While the arms are fully extended, the palm is held tight. When the fingertips are looking at the floor, the listeners will shut up. Performing this gesture, you can pronounce some unimportant words so that the gestures seem natural. If you need, figuratively speaking, to reconcile a noisier audience, then the gesture proposed above is slightly modified.

The gaze is held directly above the heads of the listeners. At that moment, when the lowered arms are fully extended at the level of the solar plexus, fingers need to be moved apart by about two to three centimeters from each other and with such a hard palm as if to press the space in front of you. Hands are straight, palms are stiff, and they need to be lowered from the level of the head of the listeners to the level of the earth. Slow, hard, and smooth. This gesture helps pacify the raging energies, simply put, ground them. The words are not pronounced, but the focus is on the gesture and look. Indeed, in a situation of intense emotions, people do not hear words, and it's correct to use gestures, but there is a concentration on the gesture and the look.

You can apply these little secrets of managing your audience during public speaking. If you decide to apply, then remember ethics - this knowledge can only be used to good. For manipulating people for selfish purposes, there is usually a consequence.

Chapter 13: Deliver Your First Speech

Start by giving speeches to a small audience during minor occasions. You can organize a small group with 4-5 members with the same interest and practice giving speeches. Or participate in class discussions because this will give you the opportunity to deliver brief speeches.

Doing so would give you a beneficial experience and develop your communication skills through time. The truth is, great speakers started will small audiences.

Manner of Delivery

Begin with a powerful, striking statement. Keep it simple and concentrate on the main points. Choose only the beneficial facts and avoid giving too much information. Your time is limited so make every word count.

Show interest in your topic. Don't make the audience feel that you are there because it is a need or a task that you are merely obliged to complete. Make it obvious that you are eager to share what you know. Believe that your discussion is beneficial and the audience will learn from it.

Exude professionalism and confidence. The audience expects a speaker who has something good to say. Make them feel at ease and your presentation will be memorable.

Be yourself. Don't fake it. If you don't know something, admit it. Honesty will not be a cause of embarrassment; you will rather earn their respect. Spice your speech up with humor. Everyone loves a speaker who laughs with his audience once in a while.

This is the easiest way to build rapport and create a friendly environment. Be careful on adding humor on the discussion. Avoid laughing at one individual or a group in the audience just for the sake of humor. Make it wholesome or in a manner that you're best with, without hurting the feelings of anyone.

Your attitude will set the mood of the audience. You don't expect them to be delighted by your presentation if you lack enthusiasm and energy. Positive energy comes from within. We don't attract it; we create it. Then it automatically radiates to the listeners. Be enthusiastic and speak like what you're saying is one of the most important things in the world.

Never start your speech by asking for an apology for stuttering or technical difficulty. You're not there to ask for their sympathy. You are on that stage to influence them, to gain their agreement and stir their minds with brand new ideas.

A series of deep inhale- exhales will slow your heart rate. It is best that you drink sufficient water before delivering your speech.

Appearance

Your message of course is the most important part of your presentation. However, your appearance will create a good impression and make you win the audience's attention. The first 5-10 seconds of your stage appearance is a crucial part since this early you should be able to establish a positive image and convince them to buy you as the speaker.

Looking professional and credible will encourage or even make them feel excited about listening to what you will say. Wear an outfit that makes you feel and look good. It should also be appropriate for the occasion. Since you will be standing for what seems like a long time, it is best that you wear shoes that make you feel comfortable.

A worried look and a frowning face will not be of help so don't plan to do any of these two. Relax and enjoy the moment.

Posture

Support your words with the appropriate body language. Hand gestures and facial expressions add emphasis to your speech. Be mindful about your posture.

All eyes are on you so be careful not to slouch or lean on the wall, to avoid creating a negative impression. Dancing around or playing with your hands while laying down your points will be taken as a sign of being nervous.

You don't want the audience to notice that you feel that way. Do away with these mannerisms. A smile and an erect posture is a great way to begin your presentation.

Voice

Speak with clarity. Your voice is your medium in presenting your ideas so make sure that it is audible and clear. Use the microphone to your advantage. If you're talking to a big audience in a wide venue, it is best to ask them if they can hear you well.

Technology

Consider the use of slide presentations for this will enhance your main points and would likely to get the attention of the audience. Use images that will elaborate or explain some difficult part of the discussion. Be careful not to stuff your slides with unnecessary graphics or images.

This might distract their attention and you'll end up with an audience who is more focused on the graphics rather than your messages.

Make the font visible. Do not put lengthy paragraphs in one slide. Main points marked with bullets or a brief outline is enough.

Do not rely too much on your Power Point presentation as this is only used in highlighting your points or showing helpful figures.

Giving handouts is also an effective tool in emphasizing essential points. Make sure that you provide everyone with the materials. Otherwise, they're concern will be shifted to getting their own or develop sentiments that they less valued.

Feedback and Continuous Experience

Don't be afraid to receive criticism. Honest feedback is just exactly what you need in order for you to excel in this craft and do better the next time.

Mastery in public speaking is not achieved through single presentation. It requires gaining a constant engagement in public speaking activities, be it class presentation, business meetings, or a simple chat with small organizations.

Watching videos of known speakers and taking note of the things that you like about the presentation will be helpful. Listening attentively to the speech of your boss or even the presentation of your classmate is a good way of being an excellent speaker. Rule: you will not be a good speaker if you are not a good listener.

You will learn more from your experiences rather than from books so gain a lot of experience and make it memorable.

Chapter 14: Other Factors to Consider in Speech Preparation

Here are some other factors to consider when preparing your speech.

☐ **Visual aids:** It has become common practice to accompany a speech with visual aids, such as PowerPoint presentations. The advantage of such a tool is that it lends visual impact to whatever you are talking about, and saves audience members from asking you to repeat or spell something out.

As with your opening statement, however, be sure to paraphrase whatever is projected on your screen. There is nothing worse than attending a speech or lecture where the speaker reads out their own PowerPoint presentation verbatim.

It is also insulting, implying that the audience can't read. Equally insulting, it tells your audience that you haven't adequately prepared for your speech and have therefore wasted their time.

Instead of presenting the words: "Once upon a time, a little blond girl named Goldilocks took a walk in the woods and found a cottage where three bears lived..."

Your written visuals should read something like:

- Goldilocks: blond girl

- Lost GPA and cellphone while hiking in the boonies

- Cottage inhabited by family of bears (genetically modified to be sapient)

Your speech, however, should not sound like a list. It should come out as a smooth delivery, as if you were telling a story. While the list above is an obvious exaggeration, it is meant to show that you don't have to mention everything you've written on it.

That said, not all speeches need to be accompanied by visuals. Martin Luther King made some of the greatest speeches without using any. If your speech has more visuals than actual information, then you definitely need to do more research on your topic.

☐ **Transitions:** A common mistake people make when giving speeches is failing to warn their audience of a transition. Readers know when a story or topic will change because of a different font, a page break, or even a new chapter. They can also go back to a previous page or chapter to look something up.

Listeners do not have this luxury, however, so they also need cues in order to keep up.

If you are connecting two related issues, be sure to use words or phrases like: additionally, again, also, coupled with, for example, for instance, furthermore, in fact, indeed, likewise, moreover, similarly, specifically, etc.

If you are contrasting different issues, however, use the following: although, besides, but, comparatively, conversely, however, nevertheless, on one hand, on the contrary, on the other hand, yet, etc.

When using these transition words, however, be sure to modulate your tone. Body language also helps to emphasize the transition, such as pointing your finger up in the air when you say "additionally," "but," "except for," and so on.

☐ **Silence:** They say that silence is golden. This is especially true when giving speeches, for silence can add weight, meaning, and emphasis to your message. Speeches given without pauses are as bad as those given in a monotone, for it tells your audience that you do not care about their reaction, if any, to whatever it is you're saying.

Pauses can also serve as transitions, as well as break up your speech into smaller, more manageable segments. In doing so, they can improve your audience's ability to keep up with you and to better absorb your message.

When you find your audience getting fidgety, a pregnant pause can also still the room and get them to refocus on you. The time it takes them to do that will allow you to rethink the way you are doing your speech so you can adapt accordingly.

The proper use of pauses can also help you to control the pace of your delivery, giving you time to think ahead to the next part of your speech. If you find yourself starting to panic, you can also take a deep breath to calm your nerves, check your notes, or even take a sip of water to buy yourself more time.

Use such "break" pauses judiciously, however. Time your pauses at an important part of your delivery. Instead of saying "Once upon..." (pause) "... a time," say "Once upon a time..." (pause).

If you are trying to convince people about something, pauses can also help to heighten emotion. A statement such as, "How would you feel if you were forced to flee your own country?" without a pause before moving onto your next sentence, excludes your audience and prevents them from becoming emotionally involved.

An even better way to say that last sentence would be to use two pauses:

"How would you feel..." a pause at this point forces your audience to pay attention if they want to know what it is you want them to feel.

"... if you were forced to flee your own country?" (now a longer pause)

The first pause draws them in, while the second draws out an emotional reaction.

Pauses can also be used to emphasize a point, such as "I believe we can cure cancer in the next two years..." (pause)

If you want to tell a joke or share something funny, pauses are a definite must. Pauses, in such cases, do give greater power to a punch line, and should therefore be used carefully.

☐ **Constantly monitor your audience:** No matter how well you know your topic, or how fascinating you find it, you cannot take it for granted that your audience feels the same way. You have to constantly gauge their reactions to find out if you've left them behind, or if you've said something they might find objectionable.

Your main focus should therefore be on your audience, not on your visuals or on your notes.

If you find most of your audience members yawning, for example, step up the pace or skip information your speech can do without. If only one or two are yawning, then try to make eye contact, a way of saying, "Hey, I see you nodding off there!"

Even if your entire audience is engaged, be sure to maintain eye contact with several of them. It reminds them that you are actually talking to them and not to yourself. It also keeps them on their toes, for who can maintain eye contact with someone else and let their minds wander?

If your audience's attention starts to wander, gauge the situation. You could be talking too fast or too slow. If they look puzzled, you could have glossed over information that could have clarified something. If you're unsure, lower your voice. If they're still with you, some of your audience members will ask you to speak up.

This will let you know that some of them are still interested in your speech. It will also give you an opportunity to interrupt yourself and ask your audience where you've gone wrong. Once they tell you, thank them, adapt accordingly, and continue with your speech.

Think of your audience as your mirror and their reactions as your guidance system. When you're watching TV and the loud commercials come on, you lower the volume. When they put on some annoying ad, your eyes roll up and you sigh.

So keep an eye out for your audience's reactions. What kind of faces are they showing you?

Some speeches are meant to be a one-way form of communication. Others are meant to be two-way, in which the speaker genuinely wants audience participation and receives it. Whatever your case may be, always make sure to constantly monitor your audience.

☐ **Closing statements for speeches meant to convince or sell:** To increase audience participation and involvement, you need to constantly use closing statements. These are phrases which demand a reaction from the person you are talking to, and are a vital sales tool.

Examples of closing statements include, "Wouldn't you agree?" "Don't you think so?" "Isn't that great?"

If your speech is meant to convince or to sell something, it is important to constantly pepper your talk with these closing statements, followed by nods on your part. This is tricky, because you are not looking for immediate agreement from your audience.

You must therefore pause very briefly after each closing statement: long enough to nod at your audience, but not long enough to give anyone a chance to speak up.

This is called **mirroring** or **conditioning**, and is a favorite trick of stage magicians. The trick lies in implanting the word "$_{yes}$" into your audience's minds by constantly throwing closing questions at them while answering it yourself non-verbally. Since people have an innate follow-the-leader mentality, they will eventually start "mirroring" your nods with their own, even if they're not aware of it.

You'll know if you've succeeded when more and more of your audience members start nodding whenever you throw your closing questions at them.

☐ **Avoid rhetorical questions:** With very rare exceptions, be careful to avoid rhetorical questions, like "Have you ever wondered?" "Have you ever wished for?" Unless you actually have an answer to these questions, or unless such questions play an essential role in your speech, it's best to just stay clear of them.

By their very nature, rhetorical questions either cannot be answered or are not meant to have an answer. As such, not only can they be annoying to the audience, they can also distract them from listening to you.

It's like asking people not to think about green monkeys. Once you plant the idea in their heads, they can't get it out. If you ask your audience a rhetorical question that doesn't annoy them, then their minds are likely to follow that train of thought. Once they do that, they're no longer with you.

If you're doing a speech on setting up a business or handling debts, then questions like "Have you ever wanted to set up a business?" or "How do you think it would feel like to be free of a mortgage?" do not qualify as rhetorical questions.

But a question such as "Have you ever wished for the moon?" most certainly is. Unless you're selling timeshare on the moon, that is.

Chapter 15: Promoting Your Business

We as a whole realize that informal exchange is the best and best promoting. Individuals encounter your administration or item, similar to what they experience and inform others regarding you. The main issue with this is it happens sporadically between two people or little gatherings along these lines taking a great deal longer the get the word out and construct your notoriety.

There is an approach to supercharging the informal procedure by getting significantly more individuals encountering your administration or item at one time, and it includes open talking. I know you would preferably kick the bucket than stand up before a gathering and talk. Be that as it may, stay with me and you very well might alter your opinion when you consider the advantages of advancing your business with open talking without expense to you.

Why is Open Speaking So Successful As a Business Special Apparatus?

It allows your group of onlookers to encounter your ability and your identity very close as it's been said. If they like what they hear and see and on the off chance that they feel an association with you they will either procure you and inform the world concerning you and your administration.

Step by step instructions to Continue

In each city, there are numerous affiliations, administration clubs, care groups, therapeutic services associations and so forth in critical need of speakers for their month to month gatherings or yearly feasts. Check your phone catalog or provincial group index distributed by your neighborhood daily paper for gathering names and contact data.

When you have chosen the gatherings you might want to present to, call them and request the name of the individual accountable for coating up speakers. They will be cheerful to get notification from you as their occupation is troublesome and they will value your offer to talk for nothing out of pocket.

1. Diagram your discussion to the individual accountable for getting speakers.

2. Push how your presentation will advantage their individuals.

3. Set up your display to take care of an issue for your audience members. Propose stable arrangements.

4. Put your presentation subject as a " How to" title.

Cases: How to Spook Confirmation Your Kids.

Five Approaches to Shield Your PC from Programmers

5. Try not to make your discussion excessively self-special. This will kill your gathering of people. Maybe a couple of references to your business amid your discussion will be okay. Abstain from having more than that.

6. Ensure you give extraordinary down to earth, useable data.

7. Suit your point to the gathering. If you have a PC administration business, and you are conversing with a P.T.A. bunch, an excellent talk would be " Ten Approaches to Shield Your Kids From Tyke Predators on the Web."

8. Be eager about your theme. Energy is infectious and influential.

9. Use cleverness inside your discussion. On the off chance that you can't recount a funny story then gather and utilize amusing jokes identified with your subject.

* To get a free duplicate of my 35Best Jokes mailto:oneliners@sendfree.com

10. Close to the end of your presentation welcomes your group of onlookers to get a duplicate of a tip sheet you arranged and conveyed with you identified with your subject. Toward the end of the tip sheet put your contact data in addition to an announcement welcoming them to duplicate the tip sheet and offer it to anybody they think would be intrigued. All you ask is that they copy the tip sheet as is with your contact data in thoughtfulness.

11. You can likewise show on the tip sheet and orally that you are accessible to address any gathering they think would profit by your message.

12. Have your business card and any pertinent limited time material as a component of a freebie for a group of onlookers individuals. Welcome, them to get a bundle before they clear out.

13. Toward the end of your discussion say, " I will be happy to stay around at the finish of the night to answer any inquiries you may have.

14. On the off chance that you have an on-line pamphlet or a different report identified with the point of the night offer to send them a duplicate if they would leave either their business card or their email address. When you return home to ensure you send them what you advertised. Make certain to keep their email addresses on the document for future contact.

15. If you are great, the word will spread, and you will begin inspiring calls to talk. When this happens, you can start charging an expense for your talking administrations.

When I started charging for my talking policies, I did 50 in one year for $200 per discourse. Presently I do 40 or 50 a year for amongst $1800 and $2500 in addition to costs. I get generously compensated to talk regardless I profit from verbal promoting.

Conclusion

On the off chance that you have a trepidation of open talking don't give it a chance to prevent you from profiting from the limited time benefit of giving presentations. Recall that you just beat your fears by defying them head on. When you vanquish your apprehension of talking openly, you will have available to you an intense and viable reputation apparatus. Also, you won't have top pay out one penny.

Chapter 16: Public Speaking – How to Appearand Be Confident Onstage

Summary

Public speaking is a nightmare for most people. Here is what you can do to make the best at it if the chance arises.

Public Speaking – How to Appear and Be Confident Onstage

You would be surprised to know that a lot of eminent public speakers still mention about their stage-fright. We are social animals, but when it comes to facing a crowd in a commanding manner, many of us falter. Here are some points that can help you do better:-

1. The first thing you must do is practice. You must go through the topic you are going to speak about several times over. If you are called to speak on

something extempore, this can't be done, but let us assume you have a notice, however short it is. Rehearse the speech in your mind.

2. While rehearsing, you must actually mentally place yourself on the stage.

Don't think about the empty walls that surround you right now, think about the several eager ears that will be sitting in front of you. This puts new pep into your practicing and actually motivates you to practice more.

3. The first sentence is your ice-breaker here. If you deliver it well, the rest of the speech usually becomes a breeze. Make sure you practice it the most.

4. Now, keep one thing in mind. Your audience is very much interested in hearing what you have to say. They aren't going to heckle you. In fact, they will encourage you by giving applause or a laugh at the right moment. Understand that your audience is with you – they are

probably considering you are superior to them because you are the one talking.

5. Always keep a few great jokes ready, especially to tell them at the start. When you see your audience laughing at what you say, you feel more relaxed. The nervousness tides away.

6. Focus on what you are trying to say, not on your words. This is extremely important. It is all right if you slur some words or if some words come out of your mouth ungrammatically. What's important is that your message should be conveyed.

7. If you make a mistake or if you have a slip-up, there is no need to be apologetic. Your audience is human; they understand such things. In most cases, people don't even notice small speech errors.

8. Keep practicing. Don't let any opportunity to speak to a crowd pass you by.

When you speak more, you are able to deliver better.

Think of yourself as important and you will be able to do a lot better. For that, you will need confidence; you will need to know your self-worth.

CHAPTER 17: TIPS FOR PUBLIC SPEAKING

Public speaking is the ultimate test of confidence whether you are the CEO of a Fortune 500 company or a student giving a book report in a high school English class. Professional acts and entertainers feel just as nervous about giving a speech at their best friend's wedding as you do. Thankfully for all of us, there are a number of things that you can do to make sure that your next public ramble goes on without a hitch regardless of how nervous you are.

Prepare

The first step to being a great public speaker is to plan properly. You do not just need to write your speech or presentation, but you need to write it coherently. When you are writing a speech, you need to be clear and concise because your audience only has one chance to take in what you are saying. It is also important to be courteous. While you may want to tell a joke in an attempt to ease the crowd, think both about what situation you are in and what kind of light hearted humor you want to bestow upon them. Test it out on friends or colleagues to get an opinion on whether or not it is appropriate so that you can avoid any awkward moments. You also want to combine what you want to say with what your audience is interested in hearing about; in other words, be relevant and be coherent. The final tip you should consider when planning your next talk is to be as complete as possible. Do not leave big open ends when you could answer them and do not include information that could lead your listeners down an unrelated path

Grab Their Attention

Once you have your speech written, you want to go the extra mile to grab their attention. One of the most common pieces of advice for public speaking is to keep it simple. By keeping your content and your language simple, you can make it accessible to everyone in the room no matter what their knowledge level is which is going to prevent any quiet sobs as someone in the audience fails a level of Candy Crush instead of listening intently to your speech. A great way to grab their attention if you are speaking at a conference or event is to get create an interesting title. The title will set you apart from other speakers, make you more memorable and draw more interested people to your audience. A great title will bring your audience hungry for more information. Finally, you should start your speech with a snappy introduction. Come up with a shocking fact or figure that will grab their attention from the start. A great beginning will keep your audience hanging on until the very end.

Practice

Once your speech is titled, written and free of any inadvertently offensive content, you will need to practice your speech. The best way to give a great speech is to practice it so many times that you practically have it memorized. When you practice, you should experiment with the way you give your speech. You can try different tones of voice and stress different words to see what kind of effect it makes on your speech. It might feel cringe-worthy, but make a recording of your speech with your cell phone or your webcam so that you can review it objectively later to make sure that it sounds like you think it sounds. You should also be practicing your body language when you practice your speech. You want to maintain both your eye contact and your enthusiasm throughout your entire speech. You will also want to make sure that you keep your hands to yourself so that your audience isn't distracted by any wild gesturing. Another great way to practice your speech is to practice your question and answer session. Spend some time coming up with questions that your audience might have and then decide how you want to answer them. It may even be beneficial to include a Q&A sheet to the back of your speech so that you can have your answers at hand should any of those questions arise. On the day of the speech, do not stop to apologize if you have stumbled or made a mistake. Most of the time, the audience does not notice if you have made a mistake until you tell them you have done so. If you have made a factual error that does not make sense, correct it at the appropriate moment or take a moment after your conclusion to restate the fact.

Ask Questions

You were not invited to speak solely to answer questions from your audience. Your role as speaker is to inform the audience about a topic and then encourage them to think about it. The best public speakers ask leading questions to keep their audiences involved in the conversation. By asking these questions, you will leave your audience down the path of learning and get them thinking more about the topic. Asking questions during the talk will also lead to them asking more questions after the talk is over. They say that the best presentations are those that generate the most conversation when they are over. By guiding your audience down a path and giving them questions to answer, they will become more involved with your speech or presentation and they will often take more of it away with them.

By following these simple tips and cutting yourself some slack, you can give presentations like a professional. As long as you are well prepared and move confidently forward, no one needs to know that you are nervous. Remember that being nervous before speaking in public is completely normal and completely natural and that being cautious will prevent you from telling the worst joke at the next ophthalmology conference because, let's be honest, the jokes keep getting cornea and cornea.

Chapter 18: Impromptu Speaking & How to Tell a Tall Tale

What is a Tall Tale?

Before the invention of online media, movies, TV, Netflix and the radio people's most common form of entertainment was storytelling. A tall tale as its otherwise known is a story ground in some realism but told in a comic book fashion and in a believable way. It's the secret of spinning a story while making it sound believable. If you can portray this well, you'll certainly have a valuable skill set with you on the stage. These stories come from fantasy and have been passed on from generation to generation & retold on countless occasions. Folktales or a tall tale start off normally enough but soon build onto as stated earlier comic book fantasy not to mention questionable twists in the story telling. Robert Cravalho states that to portray a tall tale well in a speech you ought to anchor it in realism. He states a tall tale has realism and although exaggerated its only exaggerated to the point or border of where the audience questions what they are hearing. Cravalho's tall tale spin can be found on YouTube if you are looking for an example to follow. The start of the tall tale is relatively believable talking about a high school bully who is on the football team; the catch is he is afraid of heights which he talks about later on. Later on after in the story Cravalho ends it with the bully in a mad dash to catch him through a college campus before the bully finally ends up 4 stories high in a bell tower. The part of the story that is fantasy is the last bit which Cravalho reveals at the end which is where the bully remains 4 stories high and frozen in time finishing off his speech with an evil laugh. This is the essence of a tall tale.

Do you want to tell a tall tale?

. If you want to do present a tall tale like the example just mentioned, then the best pointers are to have fun writing & telling your tall tale because if you have fun with it will show off in the delivery and your audience will have fun listening to it. If you have writers block and you are looking to start but can't think of an idea then think about some form of conflict from your past, when this you have found one. Think of ways you can slightly exaggerate the story and also think of ways you may have resolved that situation; this can be the basis of your own tall tale story. Remember a tall tale is grounded in realism so having it partly true will make it much easier for you to find something to talk about. If you have had a lot of practice with presenting in the past, then why not include skills you've learnt in the past. Include an opening that grabs the audience's attention, gestures, facial expressions, and different voice tonalities to keep their attention. When you include a twist especially at the end this is fun for listeners to hear they'll want to know what happens next. Lastly, practice your speech again and again if you do this enough then the passion of the speech will come across to your audience and it will elevate its effectiveness.

Impromptu speaking

Some speakers prefer impromptu speaking as opposed to long durations of memorizing, practising and rehearsing a speeches and this is because it helps bring out the spontaneity factor of the speaker. Yet for many impromptu speaking is disliked and considered to be a struggle, researchers from Rice University, Johns Hopkins & Columbia University filed their findings that people's ability to speak and write are controlled by two separate areas of the brain. They state this is why people write differently from how they speak, when we write a speech ideas are edited more slowly using less conversational phrases but when we speak in the moment no or little previous practise on the speech has occurred so the speech doesn't sound edited. Basically, this means in a practised speech we think before writing a speech and that comes off more in the delivery but with impromptu speaking, we speak before we think which is how conversation occurs.

Common Concerns

The basis of impromptu speaking is you are given a subject & you are expected to talk about this topic from 1-2 minutes some concerns people can often have been to share their own opinion on a controversial subject which they can become extremely passionate about discussing in a simple impromptu speech. Regardless this concern ought not to bother you while in many cases certain people can be selected to do impromptu speaking on a random subject in a club setting in most cases these talks will not take very long to do. No one will judge you because it is not a topic you picked and it's a skill that can have transferable benefits beyond the presentation setting. Or if you practise this type of speaking at a club then those skills learnt have the potential to go far beyond it.

4 Steps to being a good impromptu speaking

If you do have an ongoing struggle with this, then here are some steps you can incorporate into your speech to help improve this. Thinking calmly is something to incorporate here especially in a club setting, for this if you know you'll be picked later on in the session then think about conversations or events in your mind because they may be of help later on as possible things to say. Number 2 is organized clearly for this develop an opening body & closing so take this bit from the previous practice of other speeches you might have done. Many people star an impromptu speech by repeating the question out loud to give them more time while this is a good strategy to buy yourself more time if you are more concerned with brainstorming yet it isn't that effective at creating a good powerful opener. So after enough practice begins opening as you would a speech, a quote or statement could be a wise alternative do this & then tell a quick story or make your point and this will sound off the opener effectively. Number three deliver masterfully don't forget that 93% of communication is our body language and just 7% is the words we speak so what will make the difference is what your body is saying not the words. This includes voice tonality, eye contact, posture, facial expressions and hand gestures. Also, be mindful of the filler words that can crop up like um, you know and err everybody is guilty of these in the majority of speeches made but that doesn't mean you can't dial down on these unnecessary words. Lastly learn to time perfectly. Many people do not realize how much can be said in the space of a few minutes for some impromptu speaking helps sky people to expand on what they say and for people who are more talkative it helps to reduce what they are saying so to reach the point. With impromptu speaking it is sometimes best if you use short phrases, try to avoid long sounding explanations and any talk that goes around the point you are attempting to make.

Conclusion

Thank you again for downloading this book!

I hope this book was able to help you to gain insights on how to develop unstoppable confidence in public speaking. I also hope you come away with a strong conviction and confidence in your ability to give amazing performances, whenever you're called upon to speak in front of large groups of people!

Relax, and trust yourself…

Thank you and good luck!

www.ingramcontent.com/pod-product-compliance
Lightning Source LLC
Chambersburg PA
CBHW072010070526
44583CB00015B/1421